GW01605904

The Ultimate Passover Planner

Rae Shagalov

101 Soul Tips, Cleaning & Shopping Checklists, Coloring Pages, Pesach Insights, Easy Passover Recipes, Meditations, Art & Quotes for the Passover Seder

Copyright 2019 Rae Shagalov all rights reserved.
No part of this book may be reproduced or transmitted by any form or by any means, electronic or mechanical,
including photocopy, recording, or any information storage or retrieval system, without prior written consent from the author.

Contact the author or publisher.
E-mail: info@holysparks.com

--For wholesale discounts and bulk discounts for groups and teachers

--To arrange a creative workshop or author event with Rae Shagalov

--For custom calligraphy or artnotes from classes, live or recorded

--To dedicate a volume in the Joyfully Jewish series in memory or honor of someone special

--personal coaching for help to elevate your Jewish connection & creativity

LET'S CONNECT!
Facebook.com/soultips
Pinterest.com/holysparks
Twitter.com/holysparks
Youtube.com/holysparksbooks
Instagram.com/holysparks

I would love to hear your insights and questions, and see your colorful creations, so let's connect!
Feel free to email me with questions, suggestions & pictures of your coloring at:
INFO@HOLYSPARKS.COM

SIGN UP TO RECEIVE FREE ART, COLORING PAGES
& RAE SHAGALOV'S JOYFULLY JEWISH ARTNOTES NEWSLETTER!
Go to: WWW.HOLYSPARKS.COM

Printed in the United States of America
First Printing, 2019
978-1-937472-07-8 paperback

Holy Sparks Press
www.holysparks.com

Please do not write or color on Shabbat or Jewish holy days,
as writing and coloring are prohibited by Jewish law on those days.

This is a gift for:

From:

May you be blessed with success and only good things

Holy Sparks

WWW.HOLYSPARKS.COM

© 2018 Rae Shagalov

Praise for the Passover Soul Kit

"This kit is AMAZING! It transformed our entire Passover experience this year!" -Cindy Abrams -

"The Passover Soul Kit is such a blessing, full of inspiring thoughts to help make the holiday special. Print the beautiful calligraphy to hang on your wall as constant gentle reminders to experience the joy of the preparations and the true meaning of Passover." -Reba Linker-

"These are food for thought that will help the Passover preparations go calmly. I love the thoughts, inspiration and artwork! I feel so serene as I head into Passover."

"I enjoyed the simple practical tips of how to have the right mindset going through Passover. It's got recipes to help out as well. I highly recommend this book." -Kim-

"This guide has come at a time of spiritual drought in my life, and is a reminder that Pesach is indeed a time of overcoming obstacles and limitations. It has brought much needed simcha!" -H K Rapp-

"I especially loved how the author connects spirituality to everything that is being done, and not in the meaning of a routine ritual, but more of a real atmosphere: the cleaning, the clearing, being with the spirit, being calm and in this holy wave of this true holiday." Olga Farber

Table of Contents

How to Use This Planner

Feel free to open the book wide and break the binding so you can easily remove the pages. Choose which ones you would like to put up on your walls to inspire you in the weeks leading up to Passover and surround yourself with this inspiration to set a positive and spiritually uplifting tone in your home.

Use them as they are in black and white or invite your children to color them in for you. If you enjoy coloring, color them in yourself in your periods of relaxtion – you *ARE* taking relaxation breaks, right?!!!

For best results, use colored pencils or crayons. If you use markers or paints, put a piece of cardboard behind the page to prevent bleed-through.

Prepare for a Peaceful Panic-Free Passover!

The waft of the frying latkes of Hanukkah is barely behind us.
The breeze in the trees of Tu B'Shevat have just blown by.
It's not even time to pack the Shaloch Manos baskets of Purim
But the whispers and echoes of anxiety of Passover are hovering ever-closer.

STOP!

Hold it right there.

This is the year things are going to be different.

Together, we are going into the preparations for Pesach with joyful determination, meaningful mindfulness, and the happy hum of organized, purposeful Passover preparations.

Really.

I wouldn't call myself a maven.
I'm not the best balabusta.

But, hey! You know me.
I take really good notes.
And I've asked the wise and wonderful Jewish women of Facebook (thank you!!!) to share their best Passover tips, tricks and EASY recipes with us.

This is not intended to be a comprehensive guide to preparing for Passover.

This guide is meant to help you prepare for Pesach, in a more relaxed, meaningful, and less-stress environment of love with a Joyfully Jewish, positive work-flow.

I've included Artnotes and quotes about Pesach that I wrote in many classes that I've taken with some of the very best Jewish teachers of our generation, and of course, there are plenty of stress-reducing coloring pages and meditations for you and your family to enjoy.

So, here they are! Use them in good health and happiness.

ב״ה
SPIRITUAL
INSPIRATION
FOR PREPARING
FOR PASSOVER
Holy Sparks
WWW.HOLYSPARKS.COM
© 2019 Rae Shagalov

Soul Tip #1

Work pleasantly together with your family when you can. Create a team feeling.

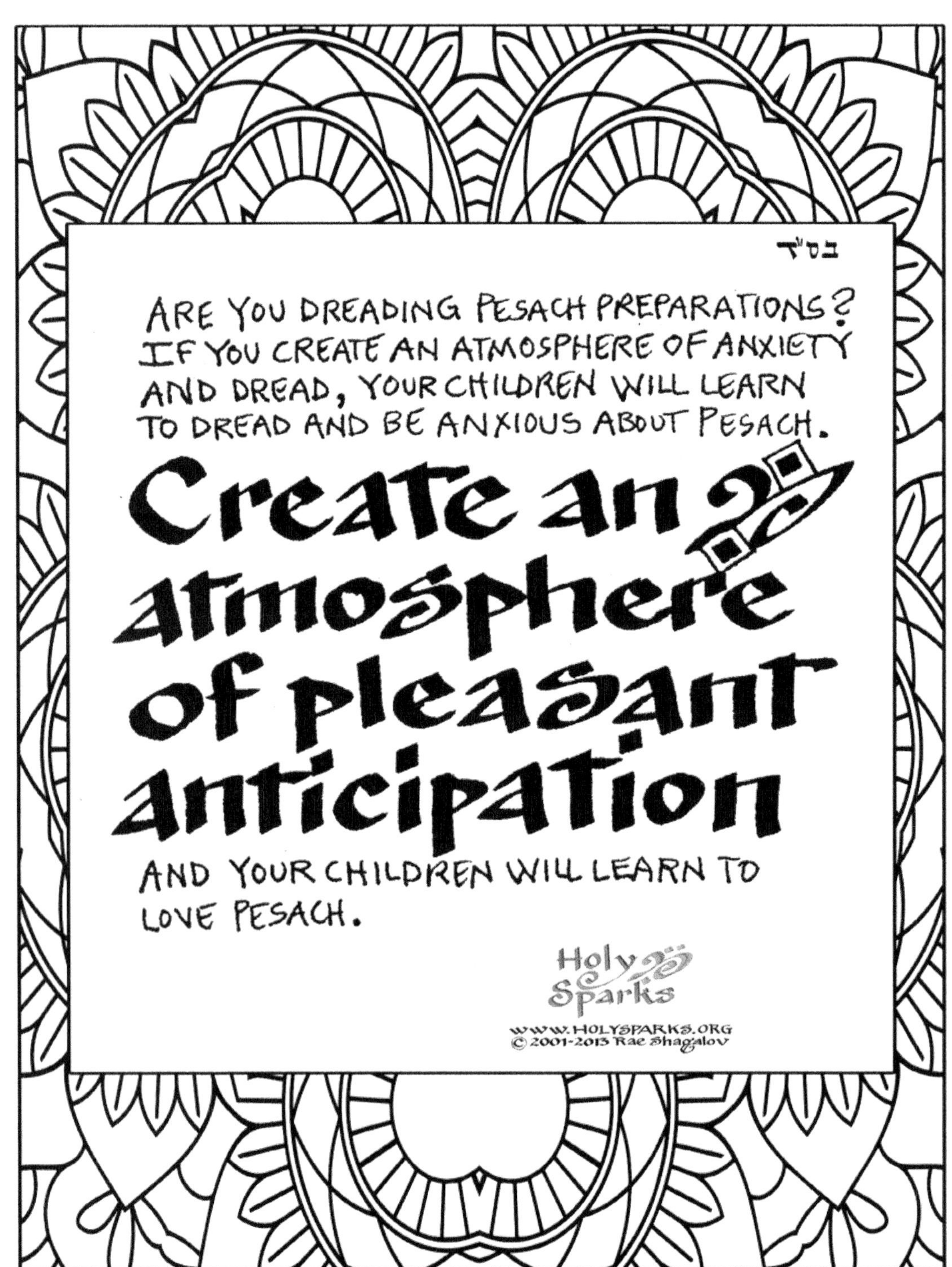

THE BREATH OF G-D MEDITATION

Soul Tip #2

Passover can be very stressful. Here's a meditation that can help you release the stress and get some instant energy to enjoy the process of preparing. The key is to recognize your stress symptoms and reactions immediately and transform them with this *Breath of G-d* meditation.

Take a short break and sit in a comfortable place.

Relax and take a few deep breaths, and let them out slowly. Imagine that you are receiving your breath of air directly from G-d breathing into you because in reality that's exactly what's happening.

Feel the joy of that connection to G-d with every breath. When you exhale, release everything that does not feel good ~ distress, pain, anxiety, fear, tiredness.

Release every form of negativity.
Just let it go when you breathe out.
Then, breathe in another breath of life, directly from G-d.

It's that simple to re-establish your connection to G-d in any moment, and to re-connect with the holiness that's hidden in all of your cleaning, cooking, shopping, and other mundane preparations for Passover.

In the space of a single breath, you can change your attitude and your life.

Whenever any form of negativity arises, if you feel tired, irritable, angry, frustrated, or overwhelmed, just breathe out the negativity and breathe in G-d.

Every breath you take is a gift from G-d and a reminder that G-d loves you, is taking care of you in every moment, and has faith in you to succeed in your mission.

Soul Tip #3

Remember to hug your family *often.*

Soul Tip #4

Keep smiling! Put a smile on your face, and it will change your mood. Your smile will also encourage and reassure your family and put them in a good mood, too.

Soul Tip #5

Try to have your kitchen ready early so that the delicious smells of the holiday food create a mood of anticipation.

Soul Tip #6

A MEDITATION WHILE CLEANING:

Soul Tip #7

Talk to G-d as you work. Say what's on your heart. Ask for everything you need.

Soul Tip #8

Share some of the insights from this Passover Soul Kit, or from other sources you are learning, with your family as you work.

Soul Tip #9

Look for pleasurable moments in the work and let them lift you up.

Soul Tip #10

Begin by de-cluttering: as you remove the unnecessary items from your rooms, meditate on what might be some things that need to be removed from your life.

Soul Tip #11

בס"ד
Plan and Delegate!
Plan and Prepare!
BREAK DOWN THE TASK INTO BITE-SIZE PIECES
Holy Sparks
WWW.HOLYSPARKS.ORG
© 2001-2013 Rae Shagalov

Soul Tip #12

Make your requests for help *respectfully.*

Soul Tip #13

Soul Tip #14

Sing or hum while you work.

Soul Tip #15

Create happiness; don't wait for it. Create an upbeat and happy feeling that's infectious while you work, as if you were preparing for a wonderful vacation. Preparing for Passover is part of the journey of leaving Egypt.

Soul Tip #16

Pesach cleaning is not spring cleaning.
Don't make yourself crazy; make priorities instead.

Soul Tip #17

When we clean for Pesach, we are searching for every bit of *chometz*, every crumb of bread and grain that is inflated. At the same time, we are searching for every bit of inflated ego, every little bit of darkness in our souls that is blocking G-d's light from reaching us.

Soul Tip #18

Do one thing at a time and complete it.

Soul Tip #19

Begin with the end in mind. Take out your Jewish calendar and work backwards. What do you want to be doing the morning before Passover? What about the morning of *bedikas chametz*?

Continue working backwards to today, scheduling in the tasks you want to complete, a reasonable amount of work for each day. Use the calendars and checklists in this planner to help you.

Soul Tip #20

Instead of giving orders, speak sweetly.

Soul Tip #21

Create positive memories of the days leading up to the holiday, as much as from the holiday itself.

Soul Tip #22

G-d says, "I want you to love me in your *mitzvot*." G-d wants us to sing our unique love to Him in our *mitzvot*, in every bit of our cleaning and preparation for Passover.

Soul Tip #23

Scrub away your jealousy and judgments of others while you're scrubbing away the *chometz* and grime. They are an internal form of *chometz*.

Soul Tip #24

Soul Tip #25

Start small – one minute, one little corner of a drawer, half a shelf. Once you engage in the activity, it will get finished before you know it!

Soul Tip #26

G-d chose YOU to go on this special Passover journey in your home and in your life.

Soul Tip #27

Chometz is compared to arrogance, so while you are searching for *chometz*, look for anywhere inside yourself and your activities where you could increase your modesty.

Soul Tip #28

Soul Tip #29

Remember to drink often so that you are not dehydrated. Eat and feed your family extra healthy snacks and meals so that no one gets cranky, and so that you have plenty of energy for your tasks.

Soul Tip #30

Don't compare yourself to others. It will only bring your spirits down. You don't know their real situation, and whatever it is, it's completely different from yours.

Soul Tip #31

Soul Tip #32

While you are cleaning out the gunk in your house, look for where you could clean out the gunk in your soul, the *shmutz* that is covering up the purity of who you are.

Soul Tip #33

Take breathing and quick little meditation breaks, like this one: Take a deep breath and let it out slow... take the stress and worry and just let it go!

Soul Tip #34

Experience gratitude throughout Passover – gratitude for having a home to clean, for having food in the fridge, running water, freedom to eat *matzah* without doing it in hiding, for having clothes to wear – new or not – gratitude for the people for whom you prepare, and the health and ability to do the work.

Soul Tip #35

Soul Tip #36

Let your inner *tzaddik* out, the holy one concealed within you to help you with your work, to serve G-d in a miraculous way, higher and higher.

Soul Tip #37

Soul Tip #38

Remember the spiritual work of Passover while focusing on the details of the physical work, and your work will be filled with light!

Soul Tip #39

Soul Tip #40

Remember what a blessing it is to be able to do your preparations in freedom.

Soul Tip #41

Compliment each of your family members every day – including yourself!

Soul Tip #42

Soul Tip #43

The more you see good, the more light shines into the bad to transform it.

Soul Tip #44

The power of thought can transform reality. Transform every negative thought and grumble into a happy thought.

Soul Tip #45

Just as the Jews in Egypt labored and toiled in the fields, so too must we labor and toil in the spiritual fields.

Soul Tip #46

Soul Tip #47

A Meditation While Cleaning

The bride is yearning to become one with her beloved. The soul yearns to unite with G-d. She brings forth souls, spiritual children, good thoughts.

Soul Tip #48

A Meditation for Dusting

Humble perfection; yearning to come closer and closer to G-d.

Soul Tip #49

Put a coin in the *tzedakah* box before you begin to clean, and ask G-d to help you so that your house will be happy and completely kosher for Pesach.

Soul Tip #50

While you examine your home, examine yourself. Self-examination helps you find out where you are and how you can be better – what is good and needs to be strengthened, and what is not good and has to go.

Soul Tip #51

Listen to a recording of a lecture about insights on Passover to inspire you while you work.

Soul Tip #52

ב"ה
Pesach is a time to leap over our limitations to serve G-d.
Holy Sparks
WWW.HOLYSPARKS.COM
© 2019 Rae Shagalov

Soul Tip #53

The point of cleaning for Passover is to remember that we are "leaving Egypt," expanding beyond our limitations. As you work, think about your limitations and what you can do to move beyond them. Ask G-d to help you.

Soul Tip #54

Soul Tip #55

Look for the G-dliness in your life while you're searching for *chometz*.

Soul Tip #56

Remember that the purpose of this intense *mitzvah* is to connect to G-d through it.

Soul Tip #57

G-d can take you out of Egypt, but you have to take the Egypt out of yourself.

Soul Tip #58

We are Jews. We just do what G-d wants us to do.

Soul Tip #59

While you are cleaning, remember that you are making a dwelling place for G-d.

Soul Tip #60

Avoid criticism like the plague of darkness that it is!

Soul Tip #61

בס"ד
SEARCHING FOR CHOMETZ
SEARCHING FOR LIGHT
Holy Sparks
WWW.HOLYSPARKS.COM
© 2019 Rae Shagalov

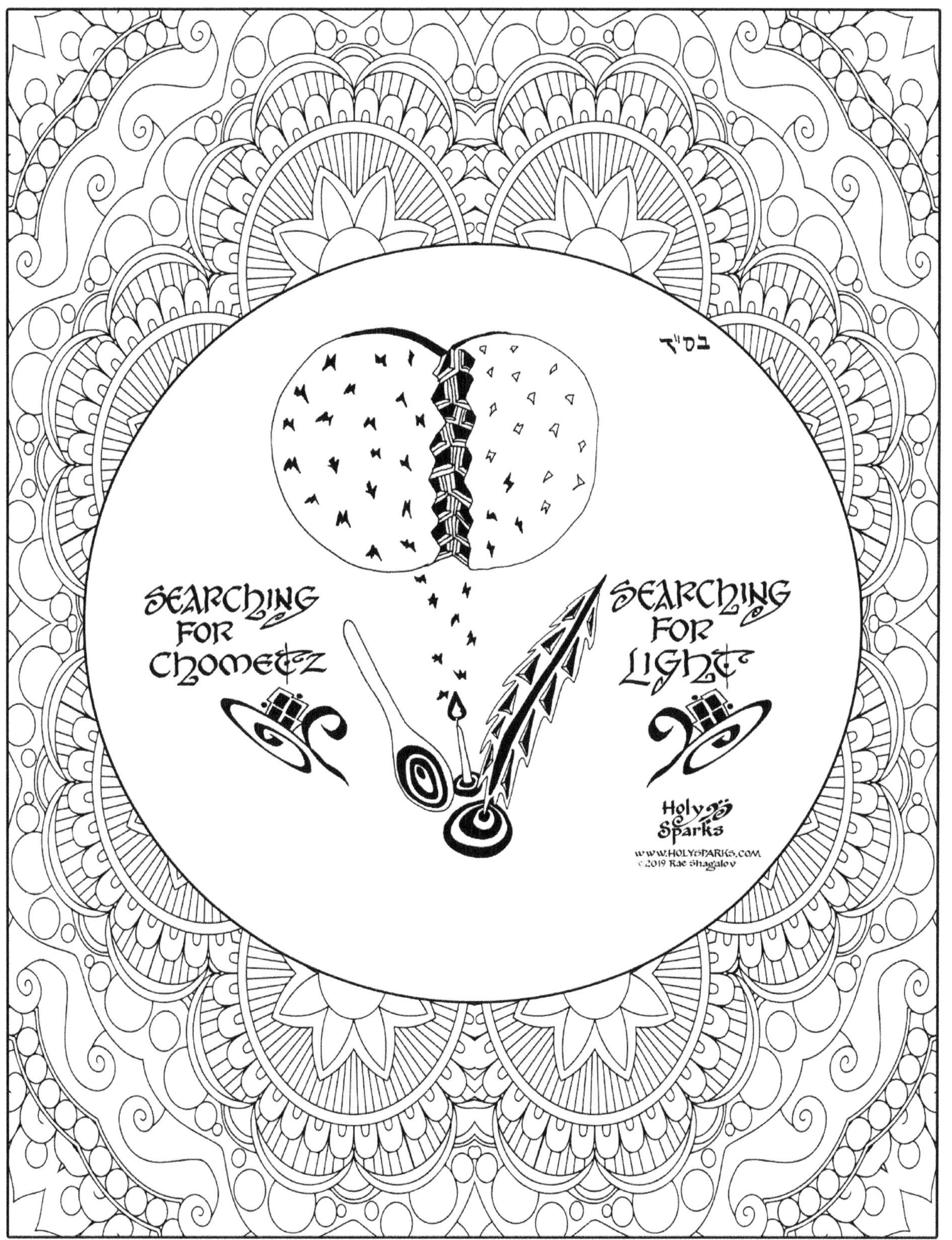

Soul Tip #62

As you are preparing for Passover, search for any dark places in your soul.

Soul Tip #63

When we search for *chometz* the night before Passover, we turn off all of the lights and search with a candle, a feather and a wooden spoon. We sweep up the *chometz* with the light touch of a feather.

We search for *chometz* – not with a harsh searchlight – but by subtle candlelight. Searching for the darkness in our souls can be done with a similar light touch, gently, compassionately searching for new places where we can let the light of G-d into the cracks and crevices of our life.

Soul Tip #64

Each day of sorting and scrubbing physically and spiritually, we're serving G-d in a miraculous way, higher and higher!

Soul Tip #65

Nourish the body as well as the soul. Eat nourishing foods, drink plenty of liquids frequently, and sleep enough to be well-rested.

Soul Tip #66

How to not get overwhelmed with *Pesach* preparations... Your calendar is your best friend. Make an especially colorful one with sticky note priorities that you can remove when they are done.

Soul Tip #67

Imagine that you are making a wedding in your home for a dear friend – the cleaning, the polishing, all of the joyful preparations – ***that*** is how to prepare for Passover!

Soul Tip #68

It is more important to be well-rested, relaxed, and alert at the Seder table than to take on extra stringencies in cleaning for Pesach. The mitzvah is to fulfill all of the Torah and Rabbinic obligations and to follow the Haggadah with the rest of the family, not to make yourself and everyone else crazy with extra cleaning!

Soul Tip #69

Buy a new Haggadah and learn snippets of new Torah insights in small breathers between your preparations. Share some of the new insights with your family as you work and at the Seder.

Soul Tip #70

Soul Tip #71

Pray for redemption with *Moshiach* while you work, and own it like you really want it ***now***!

Soul Tip #72

Listen to funny stories while you work.

Soul Tip #73

Soul Tip #74

Breathe in the Breath of Life straight from the Master of the Universe who is giving you life and strength, right now, in this moment.

Soul Tip #75

Soul Tip #76

Remember to be positive and to focus on the holiness of your efforts.

Soul Tip #77

Express your gratitude to G-d for giving you the privilege of this special *mitzvah* and the pleasure of creating a close relationship with the Master of the Universe through this *mitzvah*.

Soul Tip #78

Imagine that you are already in *Geula* (that time of peace, plenty, and a world filled with revealed G-dliness) and that *Moshiach* (our ultimate redeemer) is already here.

Soul Tip #79

Cleaning for Pesach is making room for G-d in our homes and in our hearts.

Soul Tip #80

Listen to some invigorating music that makes you want to dance while you work.

Soul Tip #81

"Dust is not *chametz* and the children are not the *Karban Pesach* (the Passover sacrifice). - attributed to the Lubavitcher Rebbe -

Soul Tip #82

While you work, think about the personal miracles you've experienced in your life, and the precious gifts G-d has given you.

Soul Tip #83

ב"ה
Set your intent:
I am doing this for G!d.
EVERY MUNDANE ACT CAN BE ELEVATED TO THE LEVEL OF HOLINESS WHEN YOU ARE DOING THEM TO SERVE G!D.
Holy Sparks
WWW.HOLYSPARKS.COM
©2019 Rae Shagalov

Soul Tip #84

Just as the purpose of the descent into Egypt was the greatest ascent to receive the Torah and to go into *Eretz Yisroel*; so too, this world, no matter how good it seems, is a descent in preparation for the great ascent in the time of *Moshiach*.

Soul Tip #85

Take another break from your preparations to breathe deeply and meditate. Yes, and another break, and several more... even if they are just three-minute breaks, they will refresh you and restore your clarity and good intentions.

Soul Tip #86

The work of the month of Nissan is to serve God in a miraculous way, higher and higher. We have to believe in our own power to overcome our limitations.

Soul Tip #87

Soul Tip #88

ב"ה
Strengthen your faith and trust in G‑d that He will help you. There is nothing to worry about. G‑d will definitely help you succeed!
Holy Sparks
WWW.HOLYSPARKS.COM
© 2017 Rae Shagalov

INSIGHTS
TO SHARE
AT YOUR
SEDER

Soul Tip #89

ב"ה
The main thing of the seder is to speak; to tell of the miracles.
THE MITZVAH IS TO TEACH THE CHILDREN. INVOLVE THE CHILDREN AND THE GUESTS CAN FOLLOW ALONG.
Holy Sparks
WWW.HOLYSPARKS.COM
© 2019 Rae Shagalov

Soul Tip #90

Meditation on Matzah

At the first bite of *matzah*, meditate on *matzah* as the food of faith (the first night) and *matzah* as the food of healing (the second night).

Soul Tip #91

In every generation, we must look upon ourselves as if we had personally come out from Egypt. The *matzah* should taste like we are leaving Egypt!

Soul Tip #92

Every Passover, we have the opportunity to reaffirm our relationship with G-d. Our relationship with G-d should be different after the Seder than it was before, and that relationship of closeness should permeate the entire year.

Soul Tip #93

The matzah itself symbolizes faith. For in contrast to leavened food, the *matzah* is not "enriched" with oil, honey, etc. It is, rather, simple flour and water, which is not allowed to rise. Similarly, the only "ingredients" for faith are humility and submission to G-d.

Soul Tip #94

Soul Tip #95

The ten plagues correspond to the ten qualities of our soul. The purpose of the plagues was to teach us to use our emotions and intellect for good.

Soul Tip #96

ב"ה
What is Egypt?
Selfishness.
G‑D CAN TAKE YOU OUT OF EGYPT BUT YOU HAVE TO TAKE THE EGYPT OUT OF YOURSELF. EVERY SINGLE JEW CAN MAKE AN INDIVIDUAL CONNECTION TO G‑D. WE HAVE NO IDEA HOW IMPORTANT WE ARE TO G‑D.
Holy Sparks
WWW.HOLYSPARKS.COM
©2019 Rae Shagalov

Soul Tip #97

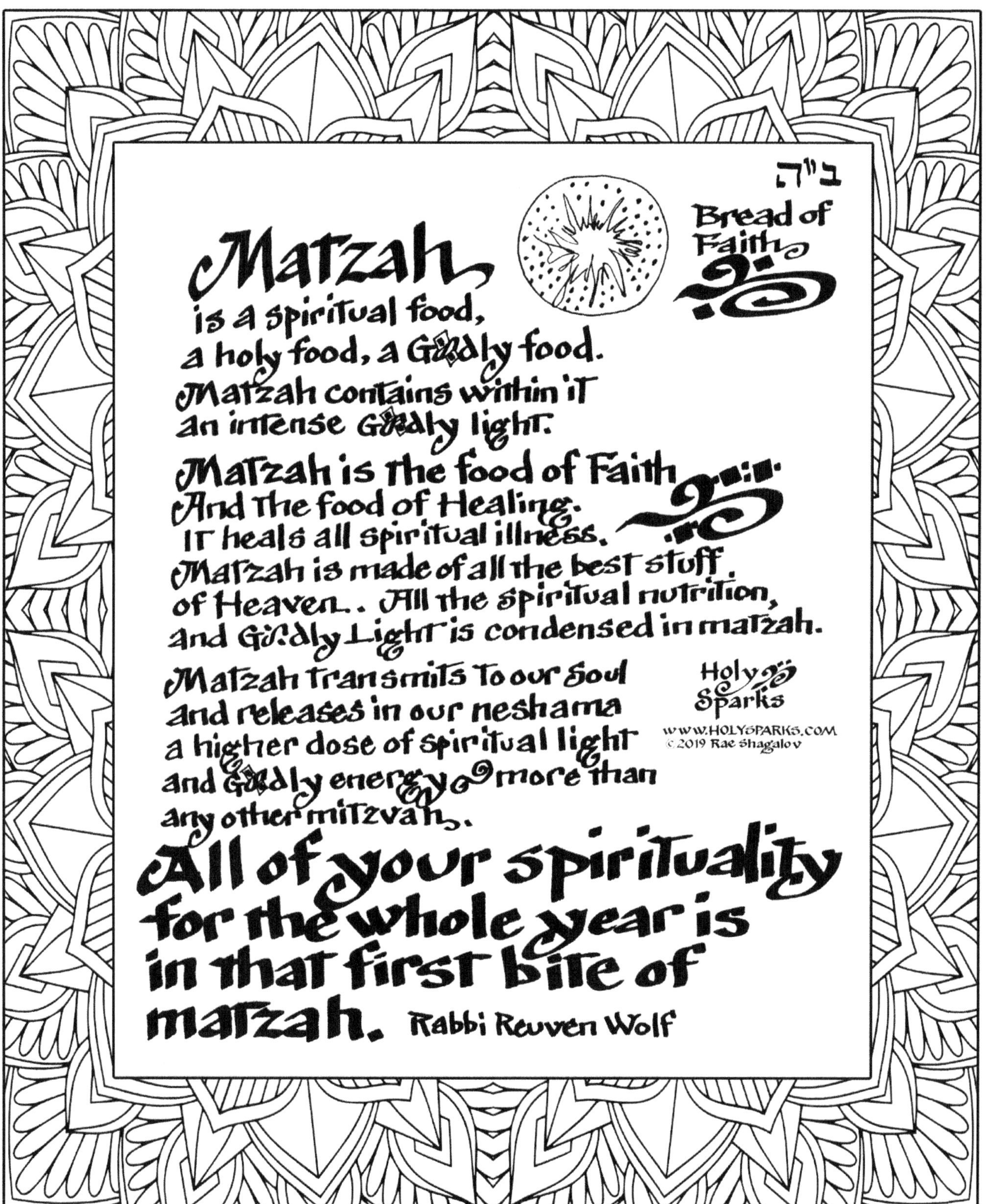

ב"ה
Bread of Faith
Matzah
is a spiritual food,
a holy food, a G‑dly food.
Matzah contains within it
an intense G‑dly light.
Matzah is the food of Faith
And the food of Healing.
It heals all spiritual illness.
Matzah is made of all the best stuff
of Heaven.. All the spiritual nutrition,
and G‑dly Light is condensed in matzah.
Matzah transmits to our Soul
and releases in our neshama
a higher dose of spiritual light
and G‑dly energy more than
any other mitzvah.
All of your spirituality
for the whole year is
in that first bite of
matzah.
Rabbi Reuven Wolf
Holy Sparks
www.holysparks.com
© 2019 Rae Shagalov

Soul Tip #98

בס"ד
IN EVERY CHOICE
YOU ARE EITHER
CHOOSING THE
RIBONO SHEL
OLAM OR PHAROAH!
WE BELONG TO THE
RIBONO SHEL OLAM.
Whom
are you
serving?
We have no choice
but to serve.
The only true choice
that we have is
Whom will we serve?
Holy
Sparks
WWW.HOLYSPARKS.COM
©2019 Rae Shagalov

Soul Tip #99

A newborn baby, at birth, is all body and no intelligence. The Jews, when they came out of Egypt, the narrow place, were like a newborn baby. They had to ascend 49 levels of intelligence before they could receive the Torah. This is *Sefiras Haomer*. How do we do this in our days? By having a desire, a longing to grow, to ascend, to climb, level by level, to come closer to *Hakadosh Baruch Hu*.

Soul Tip #100

Soul Tip #101

ב"ה
כרפס
Karpas
we dip ourselves
into the Divine Will.
BY SURRENDERING THE LIMITED TASTE
OF OUR OWN EGOS, WE ENHANCE THE
FLAVOR OF OUR SOULS WITH THE SAUCE
OF INFINITE SOURCE.
Holy Sparks
WWW.HOLYSPARKS.COM
©2019 Rae Shagalov

ב"ה
MAY IT BE THE WILL OF HASHEM THAT WE HAVE THE STRENGTH TO TRANSCEND OUR VICES AND TO LIBERATE OURSELVES FROM THE SHACKLES OF OUR SOUL, TO LOOK INSIDE OURSELVES AND TRANSFORM OURSELVES FOR THE ULTIMATE REDEMPTION.
ELIJAH'S CUP
BEFORE MOSHIACH WILL COME, ELIJAH WILL COME TO CLARIFY OUR HALACHIC QUESTIONS. WE ARE NOT SURE IF WE SHOULD DRINK THE 5TH CUP OR NOT SO WE POUR THE 5TH CUP AND WAIT. WE WAIT FOR ELIAHU HANAVI TO TELL US IF WE CAN DRINK THE CUP.
THE 5TH CHILD IS THE CHILD WHO DOES NOT COME TO THE SEDER BECAUSE HE DOES NOT EVEN KNOW THAT THERE IS A SEDER AND IF HE DID COME TO THE SEDER, HIS QUESTION WOULD PROBABLY BE: WHEN DO WE EAT?
Holy Sparks
WWW.HOLYSPARKS.COM
© 2019 Rae Shagalov
THE SEDER IS NOT JUST AN HISTORICAL REMEMBERANCE, IT IS A FUTURE PROJECTION. ELIJAH WILL BRING THE HEARTS OF THE CHILDREN BACK TO THE PARENTS AND HE WILL BRING BACK THE HEARTS OF THE PARENTS TO THE CHILDREN.
MAY IT HAPPEN IN OUR DAY.
"Elijah's cup" Adar 24, 5758
Rabbi Asher Brander

ב״ה

Spiritual Illumination

reaches this world by intense "lights" channeled down into "vessels" that restrain the lights so they won't overwhelm creation.

THIS IS WHY WE PLACE THE BONE, EGG, BITTER HERBS, CHAROSES, KARPAS AND CHAZERES (WHICH REPRESENT THE LIGHTS) UPON THE MATZAHS (WHICH REPRESENT THE VESSELS) SO THE LIGHTS ARE CHANNELED DOWN INTO THE VESSELS.

Rebbe Rashab

On Passover, we are granted the power to neutralize the Forces of Negativity which have stolen the Life Force from Holiness, by starving them of unearned light.

All physical and Spiritual existence is Divine Light.

WHEN G‑D, THE SOUL OF THE WORLD, PROJECTS HIMSELF DOWN INTO THE VESSELS OF CREATION, ORDER PREVAILS AND THE RIGHTEOUS PROSPER. BUT WHEN G‑D WITHDRAWS HIMSELF BACK INTO HIMSELF AWAY FROM THE VESSELS, LIGHT IS BESTOWED INDISCRIMINATELY AND THE WICKED PROSPER.

Our job is to draw G‑d's Light back into His vessels. This is what we accomplish at the Passover Seder.

LIKUTEI SICHOS V.32 P.196

Holy Sparks

WWW.HOLYSPARKS.COM

©2019 Rae Shagalov

ב״ה

Moshiach Seudah

As you pour the wine into your cup, pour holiness into your life.

The Banquet of Moshiach

On the last day of Passover, we bring the Divine Light of Moshiach into our lives.

Make the light physical. Internalize it with matzah and wine, good deeds and song.

On the last day, in the last hours, the power of redemption is at its greatest.

Share a personal liberation experience from your life to inspire others.

Use the Power of Passover To break out of your personal exile!

Holy Sparks

www.HOLYSPARKS.COM

©2018 Rae Shagalov

1. Wash and eat matzah
2. Drink 4 cups of wine or grape juice with words of Torah and chassidus, stories and song in between.
3. Speak about Moshiach and imagine what it will be like in the World-To-Come.
4. End with the Dance of Moshiach.

Share the lessons and inspirations from this Passover.

On the last day, in the last hours,

The Power of Redemption is at its greatest. What can you do to bring Moshiach right now?

Make a L'chaim and blessings for good health and long life and everything you need!

Moshiach is dancing with you! Open your eyes and see. Leap out of exile right into the World-To-Come!

ב״ה
PRACTICAL
TIPS FOR
PREPARING
FOR
PASSOVER
Holy
Sparks
WWW.HOLYSPARKS.COM
©2019 Rae Shagalov

TOP TEN PASSOVER TIPS

1. Hug each member of your family!
Do this first.
Tell them, "I love you. We're all on the same team and we're here to help each other." Then dance like nobody's watching to set the energy and mood for the whole process!

2. Keep it simple.
Simple is always good.
By the time you eat at the seder, it's so late, most people are not hungry. Our central mitzvah, eating matzah, is the essence of simplicity!

3. Quality time is more important than quantities of fancy recipes.
Make a few family favorites, or establish a few family favorites, preferably recipes that can be made together as a family experience - that's how memories are made!

4. Start putting away money every paycheck starting in January for the extra expenses of Pesach.

5. Add to your Pesach kitchen a little each year -
A food processor, a good set of pots and pans, or a single pot or set of utensils, knives or serving bowls. This way you can build up a good Passover kitchen with decent quality items that last, but do not break the bank.

6. **If you can in any way afford it, book your housekeeper for more time** than the usual or hire someone to help you with the hardest work for even just a few hours. Make sure you request her time early before she gets booked. Whatever extra money you spend will save your sanity.

7. **Dust isn't chametz, neither is shmutz.** Clean and organize as thoroughly as you want, but make sure you know what really needs to be done for Pesach so that you don't overwhelm yourself or your family with unnecessary stress.

8. **Think of a positive thing about Pesach every day** before you clean or cook. Let the Pesach preparation transform you from the inside out, while you transform your home from the outside in.

9. **Listen to Torah lectures** about Pesach, emunah (faith), and simcha (joy), or listen to fun, energetic music while cleaning, and dance between the wiping and chopping.

10. **Use Pesach as an opportunity to clean up and simplify your diet.** Try to stick to vegetables, fruit, meat, fish, eggs and dairy, and try to avoid processed stuff as much as possible. Lots of salads help balance out all that matzoh, too. Passover is an opportunity to feel healthy and light.

PASSOVER LIST TIPS (TIPS ABOUT MAKING LISTS)

1. **Keep lists from year to year.** What you did, when, how much, what worked and what didn't work. Then you don't have to reinvent the wheel each year.

2. **Start your list NOW!** Don't wait until after Pesach when you've forgotten some details. Start your list and keep it handy so you can find it easily and add to it.

3. **Keep menus from every Yom Tov, every year** so when it comes around to making a new menu your brain isn't all, "What am I supposed to do for this holiday?!"

4. **Keep track of how much of each thing you use** - sugar, potato starch, avocadoes, etc. Include a list of type and quantity of disposables.

5. **Keep track of how many of each cake/kugel you make.** Who likes what dessert, which recipe did or did not work, how to modify the recipe, etc.

6. **Copy or print your recipes** - with pics if possible, and put them in clear plastic sheet protectors in a loose-leaf notebook. This way you can go through several years of your own recipes and menus for ideas.

7. **Make a master shopping list** to bring to the store with you. Break it up store by store to make it easier to use.

8. **Include a list of guests for each year,** what days Yom Tov fell on, and a family photo of everyone dressed in their Passover finery (of course no photo shoots on Shabbos or Yom Tov). It will be fun to look back at your family photos and guest lists to remind you of the goal of all of your effort.

CLEANING TIPS

1. **Start cleaning kitchen cabinets that are not used often** and unlikely to have food in them, like the ones over the fridge and oven or little-used closets, like in the guest room, laundry room, or office.

2. **Do spring cleaning early, not at the last minute.** If you're going to do cleaning that is not required for Pesach, do those things at least a month before Passover. This includes dusting, painting, washing curtains and general reorganizing.

3. **Do a few extra cleaning items each day or week** between Purim and Pesach or have your housekeeper do a few extra things each visit so it doesn't become overwhelming in the week before Pesach.

4. **Chometz is not a swarm of little cooties** that climb up your walls, slide on your shelves and fly into your food. I used to think this.

PASSOVER KITCHEN SET-UP TIPS

1. **Save an hour on prepping your sink!** If you have a porcelain or other non-kasherable sink, use a tarp or thick painter's drop cloth to line your sink instead of foil.

2. **Cover your counters with foil, then use sticky laminate tiles, corrugated plastic, or vinyl flooring on top** (from Home Depot) - or cover with a plastic tablecloth and vinyl placemats from the Dollar Stores. These are all cheap and disposable, and they make firmer, easy to clean surfaces. You can also reuse the place mats or vinyl flooring from year to year.

3. **If you have the space, store your Pesach things in a portable utility cabinet** that you can just bring into your kitchen already stocked and ready to go.

4. **Never leave your peeler on your scrap heap!** Too many get inadvertently thrown away with the peelings. Train yourself to put it down on a clean surface.

5. **Don't throw away plastic bags and wrappings.** Cut them into large pieces. Peel your veggies and fruits on top of them and discard the peelings in the wrappings.

6. **Put a piece of cut foil down the center of your stove** on top of the foil you used to cover the stove top (if you do that). Makes a good spoon rest that you can replace as needed.

HOW TO AVOID LONG LINES AT THE KOSHER GROCERY

1. **If you live in a home without a garage or a spare room, clean out one or two cabinets in your kitchen** very early, by consolidating the contents in another cupboard and "eating down" all your chometz.

2. **Start with your freezer** and clear out the chometz, and clean as early as you can. Then you can buy and freeze meat and fish before the long grocery lines start.

3. **Buy Pesach packaged goods early** and have a place to stash them (see above). Shop early for items that do not require Kosher-for-Passover supervision. You can download a list each year from Rabbi E. Eidlitz at kosherquest.org

4. **Shop early in the morning.**

FRIDGE TIPS

1. **Use disposable foil oven trays to line your racks** after cleaning them. Use one set for chometz foods and then exchange them for Pesach foods. We use them year round for easier fridge cleaning, and no, they do not harm the fridge or block the cold air from reaching the food.

2. **Consider renting a fridge 3 weeks prior to Pesach** (ask the rental place for a brand new one). Then you can shop and prepare early.

3. **If you put foil on the walls or door of your fridge, wet the surface** first to make the foil stick like magic.

KID TIPS

1. **Book a babysitter for a couple of days** -what a difference! - along with the housekeeper for an extra couple of days.

2. I LOVE **this tip! Hide coins in places you need the kids to clean** - so in random coat pockets, for example. They search the coats thoroughly, and their reward is a few $$$ each.

3. **Check kids' projects** that you have displayed on walls or anywhere for cereal, pasta, etc! Or check for any pasta 'jewelry' they may have made as a project. Remember the play dough!

4. **Assign jobs to each child or family memb**er - **but let them choose!** Having some choice in the process makes a big difference.

5. **Make a system so that another family member inspects** to ensure it's all looking spick and span and chametz-free!

6. **Each child or a few kids can take turns helping to clear and serve** each course at the Seder and other Yom Tov meals. Use a written roster of who washes, dries and puts away dishes so there are no arguments. Trading allowed but write it down (not on Shabbos or Yom Tov)!

7. **Put the toys in a mesh bag and run them through the dishwasher** or washing machine with a towel.

8. **Dump toys in the bathtub for a while and let the kids rinse and wipe them** – or let them decide which ones to pack away to sell for chametz or give away.

9. **Buy some new inexpensive toys especially for Pesach** every year. Have some special toys, games or photo albums that ONLY come out on Passover.

PASSOVER FOOD TIPS

1. **Avoid as much waste as possible. Start evaluating and "eating down" your chometz right after Purim.** We're so used to "stocking up" when we shop. Avoid buying more than you'll need before Pesach.

2. **Invest in the best peeler you can afford (they don't cost much).** You'll be using it a lot and if you peel EVERYTHING, even tomatoes and peppers, like some people do, it will be so much easier and faster with a good peeler.

3. **Write out a basic menu plan** of which meat and fish dishes, salads, and desserts you'll be serving for each meal for the whole Yom Tov.

4. **Use goggles to cut onions.** Keeping them cold also cuts down on their sharpness.

5. **Chop and fry many pounds of onions at the beginning** and freeze them in smaller portions so that you can easily use them in many recipes throughout Yom Tov.

6. **You can carmelize 5-10 pounds at once in a crockpot overnight**, saute them on the stove, or roast them with oil in the oven.

7. **If you use spices, close them in a container very tightly and sealed up in ziplock bags for the next year.** You might think that they will lose their flavor, but because they are not open, they taste fresher and newer than the ones used and replaced all year.

8. **Google gluten-free and paleo recipes.** They are easy to adapt for a Pesach menu.

9. **Roast meat in a slow cooker with wine.** Simply cover the meat (and any veggies you want to include) with inexpensive dry or semi-dry kosher wine. Softens and marinates the meat and tastes amazing!

10. **Cook recipes that are already familiar** to you with a few tweaks for Pesach so that not everything is complicated or new.

11. **Batch cook!** Cook the largest pot of soup you can fit on your stove and freeze or refrigerate in batches. Make multiple kugels or larger batches of side dishes, portion them out and label them.

12. **Consider making roasted veggies instead of kugels** for at least some of the meals. Put a little oil and salt on just about anything and roast it and it's tasty!

13. Having salads on hand for munching is a really good idea – especially just before Pesach and during chol hamoed. Make protein salads like chicken salad, egg salad, tuna salad, or potato, fruit, or veggie salads.

14. Layer cut fruit in a tall clear glass or plastic cup to make a pretty parfait.

15. Buy twice as many avocados as you expect to need, and keep some of them in the fridge so they're not all ripe the same day.

16. Use one or two crockpots simultaneously so you can literally be cooking two main dishes or soups at the same time day or night and not have to worry about it burning in the oven. Saves so much time and sanity!

17. If you don't use your year-round oven during Pesach, you can use a separate Passover-only toaster oven and 2 or 3 crockpots. On Yom Tov, keep one on high and one or two on low so that you can more quickly heat something pre-cooked and then move it into one of the low pots to keep warm. The 3rd crockpot comes in handy for cholent on Shabbat.

18. Pre-cook as much as you can so that it just needs to be warmed up for a Yom Tov meal.

19. Use crock pot bags or parchment paper to minimize clean-up of pots. You can use them to create compartments to warm up more than one dish in the same pot.

20. Mashed potatoes freeze well and can be used for shepherd's pie, potato soup, latkes, or plain.

GENERAL TIPS

1. **Keep a bag of Pesach cosmetics from year to year** - saves that standing in the pharmacy consulting three Pesach guides and wasting precious time every year. But do check, because some items could go rancid.

2. **Make sure you are clear about the difference between spring cleaning and Pesach cleaning.** Can't say this often enough!

3. **Clean cars early,** and then only allow kitniyos, fruit, veggies, or other non-chometz snacks in them.

4. **Don't buy crazy packaged products that cost a lot.** Instead, eat basic, healthy foods that are chometz-free like chicken baked with sautéed onions and root veggies, fresh veggies, salads, omelets, baked or pan-seared fish, ratatouille, chicken covered in pesto, vegetable soup, sweet potato oven fries, tuna with cut veggies.

5. **Make your favorite foods first.**

STORING & LABELING TIPS

1. **Label all your foil pans on the sides** too so when you have 100 identical pans in the freezer you can see what they are immediately without unpacking the entire freezer.

2. **How to Freeze and Store Soup:**
Flat in gallon zip lock take up the least space. Carefully squeeze out the air as best as you can. Double-bag with each bag facing the opposite direction.

OR

Cut off the tops of OJ or almond milk 1/2 gallon boxes. Line them with plastic bags and freeze the soup in stackable bricks.

AT THE END OF PASSOVER

1. **Write out what you have left for the following year** so you don't have to buy any, e.g. bottle of dishwashing liquid, two unopened toothbrushes, bottle of black pepper, etc.

2. **Also, note what you need to buy or replace for next year,** such as cutting boards, a new appliance, tablecloths, etc.

3. **Thank your family, housekeeper, and everyone who helped you** with a little gift. It goes a long way!

4. **Do you really have to be in such a rush to eat chometz foods** as soon as humanly possible after the holiday? Consider going to bed early and packing up in a rested and relaxed way the next day if you can, instead of staying up late to get it all done.

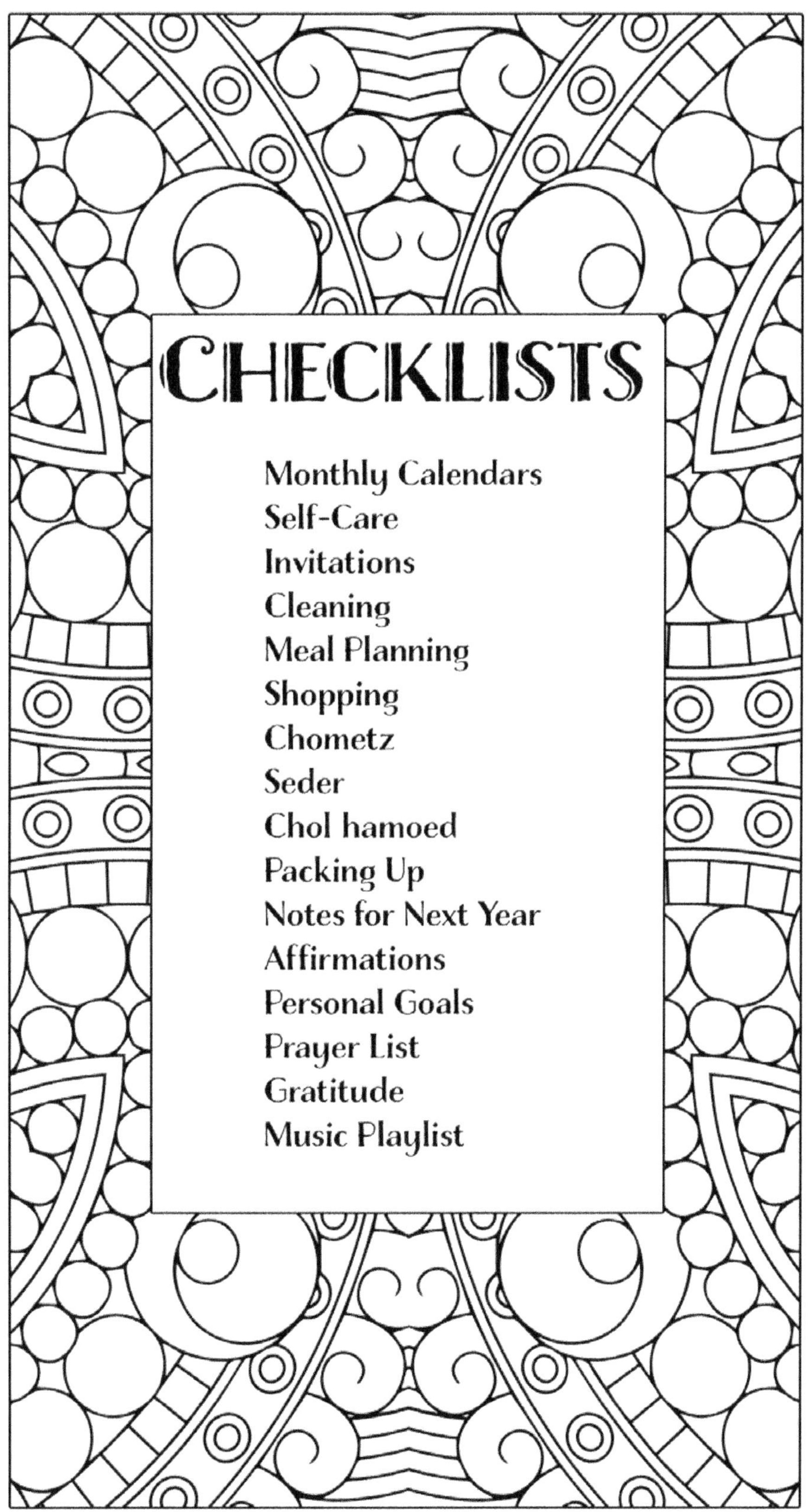

CHECKLISTS

Monthly Calendars
Self-Care
Invitations
Cleaning
Meal Planning
Shopping
Chometz
Seder
Chol hamoed
Packing Up
Notes for Next Year
Affirmations
Personal Goals
Prayer List
Gratitude
Music Playlist

monthly planner

MONTH:

YEAR:

1	2	3	4	5	6
7	8	9	10	11	12
13	14	15	16	17	18
19	20	21	22	23	24
25	26	27	28	29	30
31					

notes

monthly planner

MONTH:

YEAR:

1	2	3	4	5	6
7	8	9	10	11	12
13	14	15	16	17	18
19	20	21	22	23	24
25	26	27	28	29	30
31					

notes

monthly planner

MONTH:

YEAR:

1	2	3	4	5	6
7	8	9	10	11	12
13	14	15	16	17	18
19	20	21	22	23	24
25	26	27	28	29	30
31					

notes

monthly planner

MONTH:

YEAR:

1	2	3	4	5	6
7	8	9	10	11	12
13	14	15	16	17	18
19	20	21	22	23	24
25	26	27	28	29	30
31					

notes

SELF-CARE LIST

PEOPLE TO INVITE

MEALS INVITED OUT

Passover Cleaning Checklist

Kitchen

- Refrigerator
- Freezer
- Stove/Oven
- Table/Island
- Cabinets
- Counters
- Floor
- Shelves
- Dishwasher
- Garbage Can
- Breadbox
- Microwave
- Toaster oven
- Appliances
- Lunchboxes
- Sink
- Drawers
- Carts
- Grill
- Dishes & Pots

Dining Room

- Table
- Chairs
- Car Seats
- Buffet
- China Closet
- Bookshelves
- Books
- Candlesticks
- High chair
- Pet Bowls

Bedrooms

- Bed/Under the bed
- Bedframe
- Dressers & Drawers
- Closets
- Desks/Chairs
- Toys, Toy Chests, & Toy shelves
- Bookshelves
- Clothing
- Pockets
- Crib
- Jewelry, Rings
- School Bags
- Purses/Wallets
- Play Kitchen

Living Room

- Couches
- Chairs
- Carpets
- Mantle
- Entertainment Center
- Bookshelves
- Coffee Table
- Vacuum Cleaner
- Telephone
- Window Sills

Bathrooms

- Medicine Cabinet
- Shelves
- Toiletries
- Medicines
- Cosmetics
- Laundry Hamper
- Tub Racks
- Bath Toys
- Toothbrushes
- Tooth Cups
- Sink
- Bathtub
- Brooms, Mops, & Dustpans

Other Areas

- Briefcase
- Arts & Crafts
- Computers & Keyboards
- Computer Case
- Phones & Phone Cases
- Behind & Under Furniture
- Linen Closet
- Strollers
- Exercise Equipment
- Luggage
- Pet Cages & Beds
- Playpen
- School Lockers
- Shopping Bags

© 2019 Rae Shagalov
Jewish Art & Books: www.holysparks.com

Email: info@holysparks.com
Courses at: www.joyfullyjewish.com

Passover Cleaning Rooms Checklist

Kitchen	Family Room, Playroom	Dining Room	Study or Office
Living Room	Garage & Car	Entryways	Guest Rooms
Bedrooms	Bathrooms	Laundry Room	Attic or Basement
Closets	Hallways & Stairs	Deck, Balcony, or Porch	Storage Areas

First Glance To-Do List

Take a walk around each room and take note of the decluttering or cleaning tasks that stand out to you on first glance.

Room:	
To-Do	Done?
	☐
	☐
	☐
	☐

Room:	
To-Do	Done?
	☐
	☐
	☐
	☐

Room:	
To-Do	Done?
	☐
	☐
	☐
	☐

Room:	
To-Do	Done?
	❑
	❑
	❑
	❑

Room:	
To-Do	Done?
	❑
	❑
	❑
	❑

Room:	
To-Do	Done?
	❑
	❑
	❑
	❑

Quick Notes

Room:	
To-Do	Done?
	☐
	☐
	☐
	☐

Room:	
To-Do	Done?
	☐
	☐
	☐
	☐

Room:	
To-Do	Done?
	☐
	☐
	☐
	☐

Quick Notes

Room:	
To-Do	Done?
	☐
	☐
	☐
	☐

Room:	
To-Do	Done?
	☐
	☐
	☐
	☐

Room:	
To-Do	Done?
	☐
	☐
	☐
	☐

Quick Notes

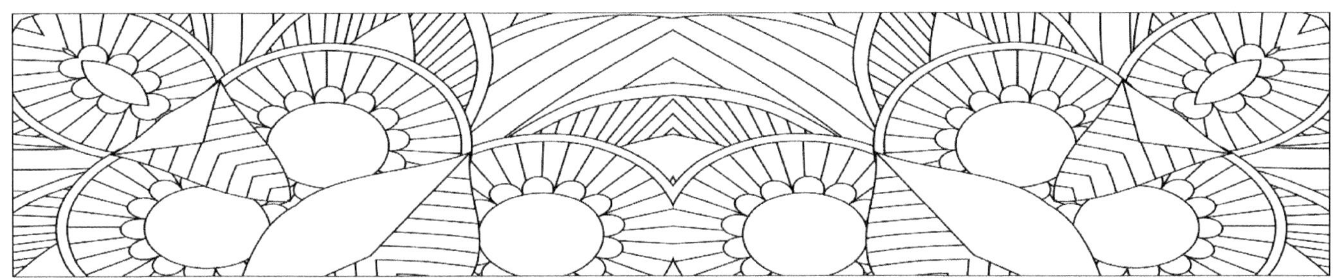

CLEANING CHECKLIST

Week ____________

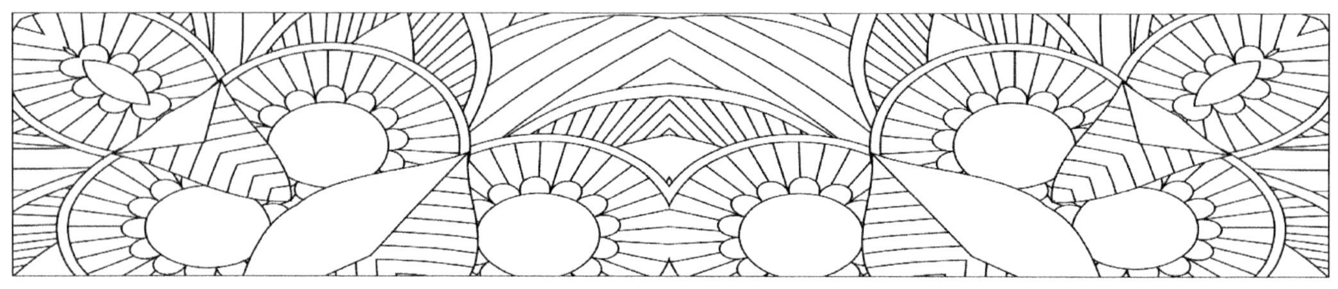

Cleaning Checklist

Week ____________

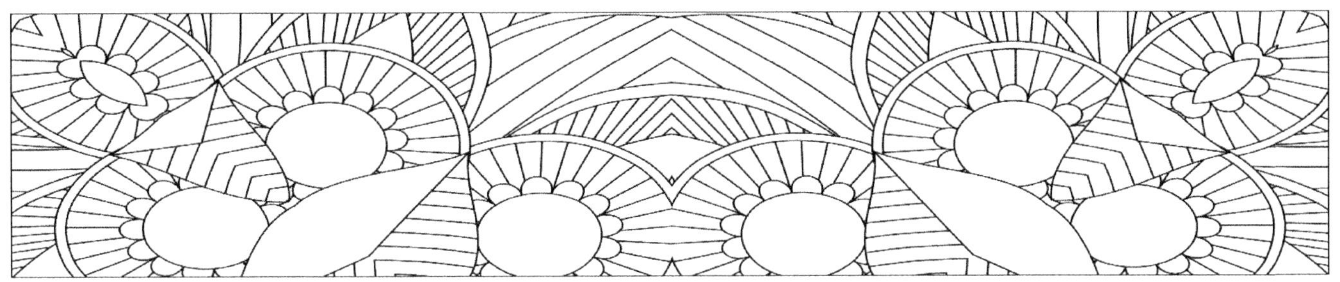

Cleaning Checklist

Week ____________

CLEANING CHECKLIST

Week ____________

HOUSEKEEPER TASKS

HOUSEKEEPER TASKS

CHORES FOR SPOUSE

CHORES FOR CHILDREN

MEAL
PREP

Meal Planner

	BREAKFAST	LUNCH	DINNER
Erev Pesach			
Seder Yom Tov			
Seder Yom Tov			
Chol Hamoed			
Chol Hamoed			
Chol Hamoed			
Chol Hamoed			

Meal Planner

	BREAKFAST	LUNCH	DINNER
Yom Tov			
Yom Tov			

Meal Planner

	BREAKFAST	LUNCH	DINNER
MON			
TUES			
WED			
THU			
FRI			
Shabbat			
SUN			

Meal Planner

	BREAKFAST	LUNCH	DINNER
MON			
TUES			
WED			
THU			
FRI			
Shabbat			
SUN			

Meal Planner

	BREAKFAST	LUNCH	DINNER
MON			
TUES			
WED			
THU			
FRI			
Shabbat			
SUN			

RECIPES TO FIND

RECIPES

Charoset

Charoset is a mixture of apples, nuts and wine, made into a paste resembling the mortar for the bricks used by Jews enslaved to Pharaoh. It is one of the items used on the seder plate, in which the *maror* (bitter herb, usually horseradish and romaine lettuce) is dipped.

2 apples peeled and chopped fine
½ cup walnuts shelled and chopped fine
2 tablespoons Passover wine

This is a very flexible recipe. The measurements do not have to be exact, as long as the mixture becomes a paste.

Egg "Noodles"

3 eggs
¼ cup water
a pinch of sea salt
2 tablespoons chicken fat for frying

Beat eggs until fluffy. Add water and salt. Beat for 1-2 minutes. Heat 2 tablespoons fat in a skillet over medium high heat. Pour entire mixture into pan. Fry like a crepe or pancake until golden brown on each side. Flip out onto a large platter and cut into ½-inch strips. Add to hot soup.

Raisin Wine

To two pounds of raisins (cut in half if desired), add three quarts of cold water. Boil mixture until one-third of the water has evaporated. When cold, strain through a fine cloth. The strength of the wine depends largely upon the quality of the raisins.

Matzah Brei for the Last Day of Passover

Break one matzah into small pieces and cover with warm water. Soak until soft but not soggy. Drain excess water from matzah.
Check and whip four eggs.
Fry diced onions until golden brown.
Stir in matzah and fry for a few minutes, then add eggs and scramble until cooked.
Add salt to taste.

Shepherd's Pie

Boil four or five large potatoes; when done, strain and mash with salt and a little melted fat; mix it with two well-beaten eggs; then put a layer of it around the bottom and sides of a deep pie-dish. Reserve a third of the mashed potatoes for top crust.

Dice and sauté one large onion. Add ground beef and cook until done. Spoon meat and onions onto potato crust. Cover with the balance of the potato; brush it over with the yolk of an egg and bake in a quick oven till brown.

Braised Beef in Wine

4 tablespoons olive oil
3-4 pound shoulder or chuck roast
1 pound peeled and sliced carrots
1 large diced and sautéed onion
2 cups of dry red wine
3 large peeled and cubed potatoes
Salt to taste.

In a large skillet (over high heat), heat 3 tablespoons of olive oil and brown the meat on all sides. Transfer to crockpot. In the same skillet, add the remaining olive oil and heat over medium-low flame. Sauté the onions and carrots, stirring frequently, until the onions are translucent (about 5 minutes). Add to crockpot with the potatoes and wine. Add just enough water or wine to cover roast. Cook on low for 6 hours.

Orange Pineapple Mango Chicken

Peel and slice 6 oranges
Juice 4 oranges
Crush ½ of a fresh pineapple
1 mango, cut into chunks
1 chicken, cut in eighths and washed well
1 cup white wine
Salt

Layer chicken in pan and lightly salt. Arrange peeled orange slices on chicken. Add crushed pineapple and mango chunks onto chicken and pour freshly squeezed orange juice and wine over all. Roast in 350 oven for 2 hours or cook in crockpot on low for 4-6 hours until chicken is done.

Tzimmes

2 pounds peeled carrots
½ pineapple
2 large yams
Bake the yams. Cut into small chunks.
Slice carrots. Cook in slightly salted water for about 20 minutes or until almost done. Crush pineapple in blender. Add to carrots and yams. Bake another 15 minutes until soft.

Almond Crusted Fish

Grind 2 cups of almonds into meal and pour onto a plate.
Whisk two eggs.
Dip filleted and de-skinned cod, sole, or flounder into egg and then coat with almond meal. Broil or fry until fish is cooked and almond meal is crispy and golden.

Almond Schnitzel

Grind 3 cups of almonds into meal and pour onto a plate.
Whisk two eggs.
Cut 2 pounds of chicken or turkey (that has been pounded flat) into chunks. Dip the meat into the eggs and coat with almond meal. Broil or fry until the almond meal is crispy and golden.

Almond Milk

1 pound of shelled almonds
48 oz. of filtered water
A muslin or cheese cloth nut bag and a large bowl or pitcher

Crush almonds with water in a blender for a few minutes until the mixture turns milky white. Pour nut mixture into bag and squeeze out the milk into the bowl or pitcher. Refrigerate and use within three days. Use the leftover almond pulp in pie crust recipe below.

Almond Pie Crust

2 cups blanched almond pulp
¼ teaspoon salt
2 tablespoons olive oil
1 egg

Mix ingredients in a food processor. Press into 9-inch pie plate.
Bake at 350 for about 10 minutes or fill with whatever you like and then bake.

Sugar-free, Sweet-as-Candy Roast Yams

Slice four yams, peel, slice, and spread on baking sheet.
Brush with olive oil and sprinkle with salt.
Bake in the oven at 400 until tender.

This method of roasting makes any vegetable delicious. Try roasting potato or zuchinni slices with oil and salt. If you cut the slices thin, they become crispy chips.

Sugar-Free Chocolate Ice Cream

2 cups almond milk
3 large frozen bananas (make sure they are very ripe and brown-spotted before breaking into chunks and freezing)
6 tablespoons of plain, unsweetened cocoa powder

Blend together until creamy. If too thin, add more frozen banana chunks until thick, or enjoy as a smoothie. Serve immediately, or pour into individual 6 ounce serving bowls with lids and re-freeze.

Pineapple Sorbet

1 cup almond milk
1 pineapple cut into chunks and frozen

Blend together until thick and creamy. If it's too thick, add small amounts of almond milk until it's the consistency you like. Refreshingly tart and delicious (you can add sweetener if you prefer). Serve immediately or re-freeze for dessert.

RECIPE

SERVES: PREP TIME: COOK TIME:

INGREDIENTS

INSTRUCTIONS/NOTES

RECIPE

SERVES: PREP TIME: COOK TIME:

INGREDIENTS

INSTRUCTIONS/NOTES

RECIPE

SERVES: | PREP TIME: | COOK TIME:

INGREDIENTS

INSTRUCTIONS/NOTES

RECIPE

SERVES:	PREP TIME:	COOK TIME:

INGREDIENTS

INSTRUCTIONS/NOTES

RECIPE

SERVES: PREP TIME: COOK TIME:

INGREDIENTS

INSTRUCTIONS/NOTES

RECIPE

SERVES:	PREP TIME:	COOK TIME:

INGREDIENTS

INSTRUCTIONS/NOTES

RECIPE

SERVES: PREP TIME: COOK TIME:

INGREDIENTS

INSTRUCTIONS/NOTES

Recipe

SERVES:	PREP TIME:	COOK TIME:

Ingredients

Instructions/Notes

SHOPPING

PASSOVER SHOPPING LIST

PRODUCE
- ○ yams
- ○ bananas
- ○ onions
- ○ avocadoes
- ○ oranges
- ○ cucumbers
- ○ potatoes
- ○ asparagus
- ○ lettuce
- ○ tomatoes
- ○ zuchinni
- ○ apple
- ○ lemons
- ○ Navel oranges
- ○ Pineapples
- ○ celery root
- ○ cabbage
- ○ beets
- ○ chives/scallions

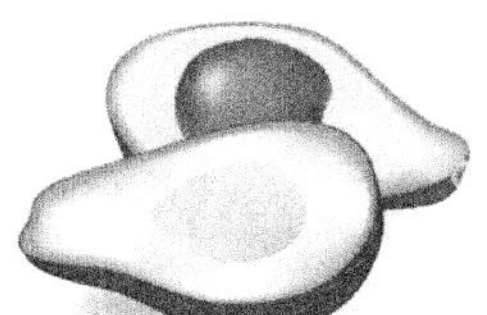

FISHERY
- ○ Salmon
- ○ Cod
- ○ Flounder
- ○ Sole
- ○ Gefilte Fish

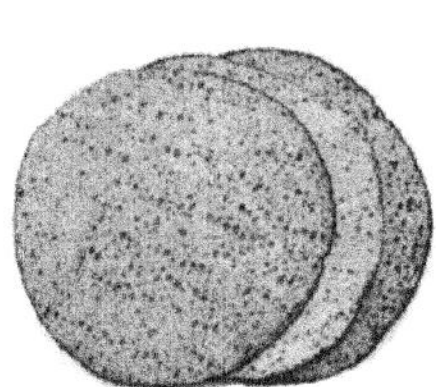

GROCERY
- ○ frozen fruit
- ○ coffee
- ○ tea
- ○ juice
- ○ eggs
- ○ almonds
- ○ walnuts
- ○ ground nuts
- ○ olive oil
- ○ cocoa
- ○ sweetener
- ○ herbs & spices

MEAT
- ○ shoulder roast
- ○ chicken (1)
- ○ marrow bones
- ○ ground beef
- ○ schnitzel
- ○ chicken necks
- ○ cold cuts

DAIRY
- ○ cottage cheese
- ○ string cheese
- ○ yogurt
- ○ milk

DISPOSABLES & SUPPLIES
- ○ paper plates, bowls, small plates
- ○ cold & hot cups
- ○ silver foil
- ○ cases of water
- ○ gallon & Sandwich bags
- ○ dish soap
- ○ ajax
- ○ wipes
- ○ plastic cutlery
- ○ toothbrushes & toothpaste
- ○ denture cup & supplies
- ○ oven trays & pans
- ○ napkins
- ○ parchment paper
- ○ sponges & scrubs
- ○ herb bags
- ○ cooking bags

YOM TOV SUPPLIES
- ○ bedikas chometz kit (wooden spoon & feather)
- ○ yartzeit candles & 2 day candles
- ○ horseradish
- ○ romaine lettuce
- ○ wine & grape juice
- ○ matzah

© 2017 Rae Shagalov
Jewish Art & Books: www.holysparks.com

Email: info@holysparks.com
Courses at: www.joyfullyjewish.com

SHOPPING LIST

GROCERIES

GROCERIES

GROCERIES

CLOTHING SHOPPING LIST

GIFTS LIST

UNPACKING PESACH NOTES

SEDER CHECKLIST

- [ ] MATZAH
- [ ] CHAZERET (ROMAINE LETTUCE)
- [ ] WINE & GRAPE JUICE
- [ ] ZROAH (SHANKBONE/ROASTED CHICKEN NECK)
- [ ] MAROR (HORSERADISH)
- [ ] CHAROSET (GROUND APPLES, NUTS & WINE)
- [ ] BEITZAH (HARD BOILED EGGS)
- [ ] KARPAS VEGGIE (ONION OR POTATO)
- [ ] SALT WATER
- [ ] CRACKED BOWL (FOR SPILLING WINE FOR PLAGUES)
- [ ] ELIJAH'S CUP
- [ ] HAGGADAHS
- [ ] MATZAH COVERS
- [ ] AFIKOMEN BAG
- [ ] SEDER PLATE
- [ ] KIDDUSH CUPS
- [ ] PILLOWS FOR RECLINING
- [ ] AFIKOMEN PRESENTS
- [ ] PROPS TO MAKE THE SEDER FUN
- [ ]
- [ ]
- [ ]
- [ ]

SEDER TABLE LIST

THE DAY OF PESACH

10 HIDING PLACES FOR CHOMETZ

CHOMETZ AREAS TO SELL

1 DAY BEFORE PESACH

2 DAYS BEFORE PESACH

3 DAYS BEFORE PESACH

KITCHEN TRANSITION NOTES

THE WEEK BEFORE PESACH

TWO WEEKS BEFORE PESACH

3 WEEKS BEFORE PESACH

PURIM/PESACH SHOPPING LIST

THINGS TO REMEMBER

CHOL HAMOED FUN

REMEMBER FOR NEXT YEAR

PACKING UP FOR NEXT YEAR

TO DO BETTER NEXT YEAR

DON'T DO NEXT YEAR

AFFIRMATIONS

PERSONAL GOALS

PRAYER LIST

GRATITUDE LIST

MUSIC PLAYLIST

NOTES

GLOSSARY

Adam Harishon: Primordial Man
B'Seder: In order
Baal Teshuva: One who returns to Torah Observance
Bedikas chametz: Searching for leavened grains the night before Passover
Bris: Ritual Circumcision
Chometz: Leavened wheat and other grains
Eliyahu Hanavi: The Prophet Elijah
Gashmius: Materiality
Gemara: 2nd part of the Talmud, Commentary on the Mishna
Geulah: The time of redemption
Hakadosh Baruch Hu: The Blessed Holy One (G-d)
Halacha: Jewish Law
Hashem: G-d (literally: The Name)
Klal Yisroel: All Jews
Matzah: Unleavened bread
Mishna: 1st part of the Talmud, Oral Tradition of Jewish Law
Mitzraim: Egypt
Mitzvah: Commandment from G-d
Moshiach: The Messiah
Neshama: Soul

Pesach: Passover

Potch: Spanking

Schmutz: Dirt

Seder: Ritual Passover Meal

Shabbos: The Sabbath

Shalom: Peace

Shechina: Divine Presence

Talmud: Compilation of Jewish Law

Torah: The Bible as brought down by Moses

Tur Barekes: A Kabbalistic commentary to the Shulchan Aruch by Rabeinu Chaim ha- Kohen

Tzaddik: A righteous, saintly person

Tzedakah: Charity

Vav: Hebrew letter

Yetzer Hara: Evil inclination

May you be blessed with a happy and kosher Passover!

All the Best,
Rae Shagalov

WWW.HOLYSPARKS.COM

WWW.JOYFULLYJEWISH.COM

ABOUT HOLY SPARKS

Holy Sparks is dedicated to spreading the light of authentic Jewish spirituality and wisdom. Holy Sparks provides and promotes Jewish knowledge, awareness and practice as it applies to people of all faiths and nationalities, regardless of affiliation or background. Holy Sparks helps spiritual seekers, particularly the Jewish people, and others who are looking for inspiration and encouragement, to discover and fulfill their individual talents and potential for service to G-d and mankind, through increasing in acts of goodness, kindness, and holiness.

ABOUT RAE SHAGALOV

Master calligrapher Rae Shagalov is the author of the Amazon bestseller, "The Secret Art of Talking to G-d," and the "Joyfully Jewish" series of interactive calligraphy and coloring books for adults and families. Rae is eager to share the beauty and wisdom of Torah through her 3,000 pages of beautifully designed Artnotes that reveal the special message of this exciting time in Jewish History.

Rae has combined her experience as a creativity and motivation coach, her talent as a Jewish artist, and her fascinating spiritual search for the true meaning of life to produce these beautiful Jewish Artnotes. Rae's books provide her readers with very practical, joy-based action steps for infusing authentic Jewish spirituality into our daily lives.

Rae offers Creative Clarity Coaching for women who want to use their creativity, discover their Life Purpose and elevate their spiritual growth. She is also an innovative educator who develops the talents of children at Emek Hebrew Academy in Los Angeles. Find out more about Rae Shagalov's coaching & workshops at: www.joyfullyjewish.com.

CONNECT WITH RAE SHAGALOV

Sign up to receive free art, coloring pages
and Rae's Soul Tips newsletter!
Go to: www.holysparks.com

There's a Holy Spark in each of us
that's hidden very well;
when it's revealed, we make our world
a place where G-d can dwell.

10 WAYS TO BE JOYFULLY JEWISH

A fundamental principle of Judaism is the protection of Jewish life. It's more important than *Shabbat*, more important than holidays, even fasting on Yom Kippur. Right now, in Israel, and everywhere, Jews must stand together in unity and do whatever possible to protect Jewish life.

The Lubavitcher Rebbe, Rabbi Menachem M. Schneerson, teaches that there are **ten** important ***Mitzvahs**** we can do to protect life. We urgently need your help to increase in mitzvahs and merits for the Jewish people. Please choose a mitzvah to begin or improve:

1) *AHAVAS YISROEL*: Behave with love towards another Jew.

2) LEARN TORAH: Join a Torah class.

3) Make sure that Jewish children get a TORAH-TRUE EDUCATION.

4) Affix kosher *MEZUZAS* on all doorways of the house.

5) For men and boys over 13: Put on *TEFILLIN* every weekday.

6) Give CHARITY.

7) Buy JEWISH HOLY BOOKS and learn them.

8) LIGHT *SHABBAT & YOM TOV* CANDLES, a *Mitzvah* for women and girls.

9) Eat and drink only KOSHER FOOD.

10) Observe the laws of JEWISH FAMILY PURITY.

In addition the Rebbe urges that:

Every Jewish man, woman and child should have a letter written for them in a *Sefer Torah*.**

Every person should study either the Rambam's *Yad Hachazakah* -- Code of Jewish Law -- or the Rambam's *Sefer HaMitzvos*.

Concerning Moshiach, the Rebbe stated, "The time for our redemption has arrived!" Everyone should prepare themselves for Moshiach's coming by increasing acts of goodness and kindness, and by studying about what the future redemption will be like. May we merit to see the fulfillment of the Rebbe's prophecy, Now!

----

*Mitzvahs are Divine Commandments that connect us to G-d.

**There are several Torah scrolls being written to unite Jewish people and protect Jewish life. Letters for children can be purchased for only $1 via the Internet, at: http://www.kidstorah.org

Listen to inspiring Chassidic Torah classes while you color at Maayon.com.

For more information about how to be Joyfully Jewish, visit:

Holysparks.com	Moshiach.net	Chabad.org
Jewishwoman.org	Jewishkids.org	Maayon.com

Learn about the 7 special commandments for Righteous Gentiles:

Holysparks.com/pages/7-mitzvahs-for-non-jews

This Publication Is Dedicated To The Rebbe,
Rabbi Menachem M. Schneerson of Lubavitch

whose teachings and inspiration lives in us, and fires us up
to try and reach heights we can't reach on our own,
to prepare the whole world for the imminent arrival of Moshiach.

IN LOVING MEMORY OF

Harav Schneur Zalman Halevi ע"ה
ben Harav Yitzchok Elchonon Halevi הי"ד Shagalov

Reb Dovid Asniel ben Reb Eliyahu ע"ה

Devora Rivka bas Reb Yosef Eliezer ע"ה

Reb Yitzchok Moshe ben Reb Dovid Asniel ע"ה

May Their Souls Merit Eternal Life

AND IN HONOR OF

Mrs. Esther Shaindel bas Fraidel Chedva שתחי' Shagalov
and Our Dear Children and Grandchildren שיחיו
May You Always Be Joyfully Jewish!

DEDICATED BY

Rabbi & Mrs. Yosef Yitzchok and Gittel Rachel שיחיו Shagalov

To dedicate future editions in
honor or memory of your
loved ones, contact us at:
info@holysparks.com

Look for More Interactive Calligraphy Books By Rae Shagalov on Amazon

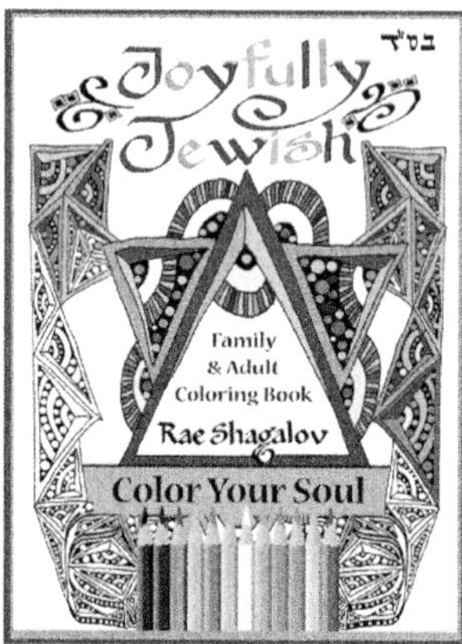

Sign Up for Your FREE Gift!

Treat Yourself to a Self-Care Mini-Retreat.

Get a free self-care checklist and coloring pages from Rae's book, *"Create Your Joyfully Jewish Life!"* at : JoyfullyJewish.com

Printed in Great Britain
by Amazon